The Other Side of Obedience

A Study on the Power, Purpose, and Reward of Obedience

By Larry M. Treat

The Other Side of Obedience

Copyright © 2025 by Larry M. Treat

All Scripture quotations are taken from the King James
Version (KJV) of the Holy Bible.

Printed in the United States of America.

"Behold, to obey is better than sacrifice, and to hearken than the fat of rams."

(1 Samuel 15:22)

Dedication

To the Lord Jesus Christ—

the Author and Finisher of my faith,

whose mercy called me, whose grace shaped me,

and whose presence still sustains me every day.

All glory, honor, and praise belong to You alone.

Every page is written for Your name's sake.

To all who have walked this path before me—

men and women who chose obedience when it cost them
everything,

whose faithfulness became light for those who followed.

You have shown that obedience is not bondage but liberty,

not loss but life.

Among them stands my mother,

whose steadfast faith, prayer, and devotion

taught me what it means to live wholly surrendered to God.

Your life has been a living sermon of perseverance and grace,

and much of what is written here was first seen in you.

May every reader find the same peace that comes

on the other side of obedience—

where the will of man ends, and the glory of God begins.

"The entrance of thy words giveth light; it giveth understanding unto the simple."

(Psalm 119:130)

Preface

There are messages the Lord allows a preacher to deliver once, and then there are messages that never leave him. They stay alive inside your spirit, echoing through every season of life. This book was born from one of those messages.

Several years ago, I preached a sermon on obedience—simple in title, yet heavy in conviction. I had no idea that what began as one sermon would continue working in me long after the pulpit lights dimmed. Through the years, other sermons, studies, and moments of prayer all began to point back to that same truth: everything in our walk with God rises and falls on obedience.

This is not a book of theology for scholars alone; it is a message for every believer who wants to walk closer to God. My prayer is that as you read these pages, you will feel the same stirring I felt when the Lord first dealt with me—that obedience is not bondage, but liberty. It is not the loss of your will, but the discovery of His.

I have watched what happens when God's people obey. I have seen lives restored, hearts renewed, and the anointing flow again in vessels that once felt empty. I have also seen what happens when obedience is delayed or ignored—the distance it creates between us and the presence of God. Through these experiences, the Lord taught me that obedience is the key that unlocks both power and peace.

This book was written for those who are hungry for more than religion—for those who want to please God in every part of life. It is meant to encourage the weary, to convict the complacent, and to call all of us back to that simple and powerful truth: to obey is better than sacrifice.

If these words draw you closer to God, if they stir your heart to renew your surrender, if they help you fall in love again with His Word and His ways—then this book has accomplished its purpose.

My prayer for this book is that the Holy Ghost would speak to you in ways that he spoke to me in writing the words you will read.

– Larry M. Treat

Table of Contents

PREFACE   7

TABLE OF CONTENTS   10

INTRODUCTION – WHY OBEDIENCE MATTERS   13

CHAPTER 1 – THE CALL TO OBEDIENCE   20

The Voice That Calls   20
The One Thing   24
Faith That Follows   28

CHAPTER 2 – THE FINISH LINE OF OBEDIENCE   33

THE CALL THAT TESTS   33
KNOWING THE VOICE OF GOD   35
OBEDIENCE TESTED   36
THE PLACE OF OBEDIENCE   38
ALMOST DOESN'T COUNT   39
THE ULTIMATE EXAMPLE   42

CHAPTER 3 – THE COST OF DISOBEDIENCE   45

DISOBEDIENCE HAS A PRICE   45
NADAB AND ABIHU – STRANGE FIRE IN A HOLY PLACE   46
ISRAEL'S REBELLION IN THE WILDERNESS   48
THE TEST OF TRUST   50
THE COST OF REBELLION   52

THE FIRE AND THE GLORY   54

THE LESSON FOR US   55

CHAPTER 4 – THE SPIRIT OF OBEDIENCE   58

THE HEART BEHIND THE COMMAND   58

THE OFFERING OF CAIN AND ABEL   59

THE PATTERN IN THE GARDEN   61

THE SPIRIT THAT RESISTS CORRECTION   63

THE SPIRIT OF TRUE OBEDIENCE   66

THE PURITY OF OBEDIENCE   67

CHAPTER 5 – OBEDIENCE IN WEAKNESS   71

THE CALL IN THE WINEPRESS   71

THE TEST OF OBEDIENCE   75

THE REDUCTION   78

THE VICTORY OF THE FEW   82

CHAPTER 6 – OBEDIENCE AND ETERNAL REWARD   88

THE PROMISE OF REWARD   88

THE FAITHFUL ENDURE   91

THE CROWN OF OBEDIENCE   94

THE ETERNAL PERSPECTIVE   97

FINAL BENEDICTION: 102

ACKNOWLEDGMENTS   104

"If ye be willing and obedient, ye shall eat the good of the land."

(Isaiah 1:19)

Introduction – Why Obedience Matters

Obedience has always been the dividing line—between blessing and curse, between life and death, between walking with God and walking away from Him.

It has never been a small thing with God; it has always been the measure of faith and the proof of love.

From the very beginning of Scripture, the Lord has required His people to hear His voice and to follow His command.

In the garden of Eden, Adam and Eve lived in a perfect environment.

Surrounded by abundance, walking daily in fellowship with God, and the reality of everlasting life, they had only one command to keep.

Yet their disobedience brought sin, separation, and death upon all mankind.

One moment of disobedience shattered the fellowship between God and man and changed the course of history forever.

Where Adam fell through disobedience, Abraham rose through obedience. He obeyed God's call to leave his homeland, not knowing where he was going. Step by step, his obedience brought him into covenant with the Almighty. And finally, on Mount Moriah, Abraham carried that obedience to the very end.

It was a moment that demanded the surrender of everything he loved most, yet Abraham's trust in God proved stronger than his fear. With the knife raised over his son, God stopped him and declared:

"...for now I know that thou fearest God, seeing thou hast not withheld thy son, thine only son from me" (Genesis 22:12).

Abraham had crossed the finish line of obedience, and on the other side of his obedience, God revealed His provision—a ram caught in the thicket.

The greatest example of obedience, however, is Jesus Christ. In the garden of Gethsemane, He prayed: *"...O my Father, if it be possible, let this cup pass from me: nevertheless not as I will, but as thou wilt"* (Matthew 26:39). In His flesh, He felt the crushing weight of the cross, yet He submitted fully to the will of God.

The writer of Hebrews declares: *"Looking unto Jesus the author and finisher of our faith; who for the joy that was set before him endured the cross, despising the shame, and is set down at the right hand of the throne of God"* (Hebrews 12:2).

Jesus, unlike us, knew exactly what was on the other side of obedience. He saw that Calvary would not end in defeat, but in resurrection, redemption, and eternal victory. The reward of His obedience was not for Himself, but for us. It was joy to Him to endure the cross, knowing that obedience would bring salvation to the world, the church would be birthed, and eternal life would be given to all who obey the gospel.

Paul, too, stands as a shining example. Once a persecutor of the church, he surrendered completely when the Lord confronted him on the Damascus road.

From that moment, he obeyed God to the very end. Near the close of his life, he testified:

"I have fought a good fight, I have finished my course, I have kept the faith: Henceforth there is laid up for me a crown of righteousness, which the Lord, the righteous judge, shall give me at that day: and not to me only, but unto all them also that love his appearing" (2 Timothy 4:7–8).

This is the truth we must grasp: obedience is not bondage, and it is not legalism. The world may mock obedience, and religion may water it down, but the Word of God has never changed. "…Behold, to obey is better than sacrifice, and to hearken than the fat of rams" (1 Samuel 15:22).

Obedience is love in action. Obedience is faith with works—because "For as the body without the spirit is dead, so faith without works is dead also" (James 2:26).

Obedience is like a race. Scripture calls us to endurance—to keep moving, keep running, keep finishing. We are not just called to start well, but to **continue** well. As Paul proved, the crown is not promised at the starting line, but at the finish line.

Just as a race is not won at the starting line, obedience is not proven until it is carried to completion.

Partial obedience is disobedience.

Many begin to obey but stop short of the promise.

- Saul obeyed only in part, and God rejected him.
- Moses struck the rock instead of speaking to it, and was kept from the Promised Land.

Almost does not count with God.

The same God who required obedience of Abraham, Moses, and Paul, requires it of us today. The finish line is not behind us; it is before us.

We must not settle for half-hearted or delayed obedience. *"But he that shall endure unto the end, the same shall be saved"* (Matthew 24:13). Peter reminds us that salvation is no casual matter, for *"...if the righteous scarcely be saved, where shall the ungodly and the sinner appear?"* (1 Peter 4:18). This truth should stir us to walk in full obedience, not because we earn salvation, but because obedience proves our faith.

In the chapters that follow, we will see that obedience is not only commanded, but rewarded.

We will trace the blessings that come when men and women of God obey Him fully, and the dangers that follow when they do not. The call to obedience is the same for every generation, and it still stands today.

On the other side of obedience is blessing. On the other side of obedience is power. On the other side of obedience is eternal life.

"My sheep hear my voice, and I know them, and they

follow me."

(John 10:27)

Chapter 1 – The Call to Obedience

The Voice That Calls

<u>Obedience</u>. That's a word the flesh hates. The carnal mind sees it as bondage, but in truth, it is the pathway to life.

Our human nature is lawless by instinct; the flesh does not want to be told what to do, nor does it desire to submit to anyone or anything. Yet it is obedience that saves us—both naturally and spiritually.

We understand this even in the natural: laws exist to preserve life, and obedience to those laws protects us from destruction. The same is true spiritually.

The commandments of God are not chains of bondage, but walls of protection.

"For this is the love of God, that we keep his commandments: and his commandments are not grievous." (1 John 5:3)

Our flesh may resist, yet obedience is life.

Before commandments were ever written in stone, they were spoken in love. The first sound Adam ever heard was not thunder or threat—it was the voice of God.

That voice breathed life into dust, shaped man in Heaven's image, and invited him into fellowship.

Obedience was never meant to be bondage; it was born out of relationship—the rhythm of agreement between Creator and creation.

"And the Lord God commanded the man, saying, 'Of every tree of the garden thou mayest freely eat: but of the tree of the knowledge of good and evil, thou shalt not eat of it: for in the day that thou eatest thereof thou shalt surely die.'" (Genesis 2:16–17)

That was not the language of restriction but of revelation.

God's Word was life's boundary—a line drawn not to imprison man but to preserve him. Love set the limit.

When man remained within that Word, he remained within God Himself, for God is the Word.

But another voice entered the garden: *"Yea, hath God said?"* (Genesis 3:1).

With that single question, Satan sowed suspicion.
The serpent's whisper still echoes through time—
challenging, twisting, questioning the goodness of God.

The voice of the enemy in the garden simply posed itself as a question, but that question attacked the spoken Word of God. Over six thousand years later, the voice of the enemy is still attacking the Word of God.
That voice has transformed from a whispering serpent to a thundering dragon: *"Hath God said?"*

That's why we have so many different kinds of churches, different doctrines, and different Bibles—because the serpent sowed suspicion into the heart of man against the Word of God.

From that first doubt came the first disobedience.

They did not fall because the fruit was tempting, but because unbelief was convincing. They believed the lie more than the Lord.

When sin entered, it silenced the song of communion.
The man who once walked openly with God now hid among the trees.
We hid because we were afraid.
Sin brings fear—but through the Holy Ghost, that fear has been taken away.

"For God hath not given us the spirit of fear; but of power, and of love, and of a sound mind." (2 Timothy 1:7)

The One Thing

They had absolute freedom and power to do whatever they wanted—except for one thing.

Adam and Eve forgot about all they could freely do and began to focus on the one thing they weren't supposed to do. Six thousand years later, we still get hung up on *the one thing.*

The One Thing
- The thing you shouldn't say.
- The thing you shouldn't do.
- The place you shouldn't go.
- The thing you shouldn't wear.

If Adam and Eve had known the chaos that would be unleashed by disobeying that one command, I'm sure they would have chosen differently. But they fixated on the one thing they couldn't have and lost everything they could have enjoyed.

Look around—nothing has changed. All that is wrong in the world is not God's doing; it's man's disobedience.

A simple act of defiance set off a chain of destruction that still touches every life today. How much better it would have been to stay on the path of obedience.

As a minister, I have watched people wrestle between their will and God's. I have seen churches linger on the edge of revival—so close to breakthrough, yet never crossing over because the one thing God required was delayed.

We fill our lives with so many things—programs, plans, emotions—but when the noise settles, there remains **one thing** that determines whether we move forward or fall back: obedience.

Obedience is the one thing that turns revelation into reality, calling into character, and hearing into doing. It is the measure of trust and the proof of love. When everything else fades, obedience still works.

Then came that searching cry: *"Adam, where art thou?"* (Genesis 3:9).

That question has never faded. Every generation still hears it—the call of a God who seeks not to condemn but to restore.

From the blood on Abel's altar to the fire on Sinai, from the prophet's cry to the preacher's pulpit, God has never changed His language.

His blessings are still wrapped in commandments. His fellowship is still guarded by submission.

The Word is not detached from His nature—it is His nature expressed.

To reject the command is to resist the Commander.

David prayed, *"Teach me to do Thy will; for Thou art my God."* (Psalm 143:10)

He did not ask merely to know the will of God but to do it. Knowledge without obedience is deception.

The Lord measures love by response: *"If ye love Me, keep My commandments."* (John 14:15)

The same divine voice that thundered on Sinai whispered again in Gethsemane. The same Word that commanded light into existence commanded flesh to lay down its life.

When Jesus prayed, *"Not My will, but Thine, be done,"* (Luke 22:42) obedience was redeemed where disobedience began—in a garden.

The curse of rebellion was reversed by submission. The yielded will of Jesus Christ became the open door back to fellowship. But that only applies if we, in turn, yield our will also.

Every call of God since then is an echo of that moment. He still speaks—not to inform but to transform. He does not shout into ears; He draws hearts.

And every soul that answers His call learns the same truth:

- Obedience doesn't chain us; it connects us to God's heart.
- His commandments are not chains; they are lifelines.
- The call of God does not restrict life—it releases it.

Faith That Follows

Faith and obedience are never strangers. Faith requires obedience, and obedience requires faith. Every man or woman of God who carried obedience to the end walked by faith.

Without faith, Abraham could not have left his homeland. Without faith, Noah could not have built the ark. Without faith, Joshua could not have marched around Jericho.

Abraham, in particular, could lay Isaac on the altar because he believed God was able to raise him up from the dead (Hebrews 11:19). Faith fueled obedience, and obedience confirmed faith.

Years ago, my wife bought me a plaque for my office. Somehow it found its way into our living room, where it still hangs today—a quiet reminder every time I walk by.

It reads: **"Faith is not believing that God can; it is knowing that He will."**

That phrase has preached to me more times than I can count. Each time I see it, I'm reminded that faith is more than hope—it's confidence in the promises of God. Faith doesn't question if God can; it rests in the assurance that He will.

Faith and obedience walk hand in hand. You cannot truly have one without the other.

- Faith moves us to obey.
- Obedience proves that faith is alive within us.

Abraham believed God, and it was counted unto him for righteousness—but belief alone was not enough. His faith had to take steps; it had to build altars, leave familiar places, and offer up what he loved most.

Faith without obedience is empty, but obedience without faith is powerless. Obedience is faith in action.

True obedience doesn't come from fear or mere duty—it comes from trust. When you believe that God's Word is true, you obey not because you must but because you know He is faithful.

That's where Adam and Eve failed in the garden. Their disobedience wasn't just rebellion; it was unbelief. They doubted God's Word, and their lack of faith led them to disobey.

Faith says, "God's way is best." Disobedience says, "I think I know better."

Every act of obedience begins with faith, and every act of sin begins with unbelief.

Faith that follows does not wait for favorable conditions.
• The Red Sea opened only after Moses obeyed and stretched forth his rod.
• The widow's oil multiplied after she poured.
• Peter's nets filled after he launched.

The miracle always stands on the far side of obedience.

Modern religion often reverses the divine order. It demands evidence before action, proof before submission. Yet Heaven still says, "Believe, and thou shalt see."

Obedience is the bridge between revelation and realization. Hearing is invitation; doing is confirmation. God does not reward understanding—He rewards trust.

"Know ye not that they which run in a race run all, but one receiveth the prize? So run, that ye may obtain."

(1 Corinthians 9:24)

Chapter 2 – The Finish Line of Obedience

The Call That Tests

Abraham is called the "father of the faithful," and rightfully so. In Genesis 12, Abraham was still known as Abram when God called him to leave his country and his family.

Abram and his household had never served God before, nor had they ever heard His voice. They served false gods and worshiped idols, but God told Abram to leave everything he had ever known and go to a land He would show him.

How many of us could do that?

God gave Abram no map, no details, only a command to go. Often, God asks the same of us. We know what He is asking, but the unknowns remain—How? Where? Why? The call is to obey even when we do not have all the answers.

Blessings come on the road of obedience. God called Abram when he was seventy-five years old. Nearly twenty-four years later, when Abram was ninety-nine, the Lord rewarded his faithfulness.

His name was changed from Abram, meaning *"high father,"* to Abraham, meaning *"father of a multitude"* (Genesis 17:5). Not only was Abraham's name changed, but his wife's name was also changed—from Sarai to Sarah.

Sarai means *"my princess,"* but God changed it to *Sarah,* meaning simply *"princess."*
The shift was subtle yet powerful. No longer was she *Abram's* princess alone—she became *a mother of nations* in her own right.
Her identity expanded with the promise.

Her blessing was connected to Abraham's obedience, yet God also made it personal.
When you are faithful to God's call, those connected to you share in the blessing as well.
God never leaves anyone out.

Knowing the Voice of God

Abraham had never served God, yet when God spoke, he recognized His voice and obeyed. The same call goes out today to *"whosoever will"* (Mark 8:34; Revelation 22:17). You do not have to be "super-spiritual" to hear the voice of God. He calls ordinary people to extraordinary obedience.

Abraham did not hesitate to do the will of God. Yet how often do we run from it?

- We run from preaching His Word,
- teaching a class,
- giving a Bible study,
- singing,
- outreach,
- or simply living faithfully for Him.

We compile excuses—but every excuse is just that—an excuse.

Paul described the struggle within us: *"I find then a law, that, when I would do good, evil is present with me."* (Romans 7:21) We want to be used by God. We want to do His will. But when He calls and asks something of us, our flesh resists. Thoughts invade, and we reason ourselves out of obedience.

Abraham obeyed without hesitation. Too often, we delay. Yet James wrote plainly: *"Therefore to him that knoweth to do good, and doeth it not, to him it is sin."* (James 4:17)

> To ignore God's call is not merely weakness; it is
>
> disobedience.

Obedience Tested

Years later, God tested Abraham again—this time on Mount Moriah. He commanded Abraham to offer Isaac, the promised son, as a sacrifice (Genesis 22:2). Abraham rose early, prepared the altar, and raised the knife in obedience.

At that moment, God stopped him and declared: *"…for now I know that thou fearest God, seeing thou hast not withheld thy son, thine only son from me."* (Genesis 22:12)

On the other side of obedience, Abraham found God's provision—a ram caught in the thicket. Obedience is not proven at the first step but at the last. Blessing is revealed at the finish line.

Faith is not defined by comfort but by completion. It is the willingness to walk even when the mountain demands your promise. Sometimes obedience will cost you the very thing you prayed for. But when you lay it down, you discover that what God truly wanted was never Isaac's death—it was Abraham's trust.

God never intended to take the promise away; He intended to take the fear out of Abraham's heart. That is what perfect obedience accomplishes: fear is cast out, and faith takes its place.

The Place of Obedience

Just as important as Abraham obeying God was *where* he obeyed God.

He could have risen the next morning, built an altar, and offered up Isaac right where he was.

He could have traveled only as far as the place where he left his servants and offered Isaac there.

Wouldn't he have been obedient? **No!**

Because that was not the *place* of obedience.

No matter where he offered Isaac, it would have only been *partial obedience—almost obedience.*

But only one place had the ram.

Only one place had deliverance.

Only one place had salvation.

Abraham's obedience teaches us that doing the right thing in the wrong place is still wrong.

Partial obedience is disobedience, and delayed obedience is denial.

That's why in the Kingdom of God—**almost doesn't count.**

Almost Doesn't Count

There is an old saying: "Almost only counts in horseshoes and hand grenades." In matters of faith, almost doesn't count at all.

King Agrippa listened intently as Paul testified of Christ. Conviction touched his heart, yet he answered: *"Almost thou persuadest me to be a Christian."* (Acts 26:28)

Almost persuaded is still lost. Almost a Christian is still a sinner. There is no middle ground.

We live in a world full of almost. Projects almost finished. Goals almost reached. Promises almost kept. But some things cannot be "almost." You cannot almost build a bridge, or almost complete a staircase, or almost finish a flight.

And above all, you cannot almost be saved. Salvation demands full obedience to the gospel.

The Death — through repentance.

The Burial — through baptism *in His Name.*

The Resurrection — through the infilling of the Holy Ghost, which is accompanied by a sign:

"With stammering lips and another tongue." (Isaiah 28:11; Acts 2:4)

Anything less is another gospel—one that can only be defined as *"having a form of godliness, but denying the power thereof."* (2 Timothy 3:5)

Moses' life also shows us that almost does not count. After forty years in Pharaoh's court, forty years in the wilderness, and forty years leading Israel, he came within sight of the Promised Land. God took him up Mount Nebo and showed him the inheritance of Israel but said: *"I have caused thee to see it with thine eyes, but thou shalt not go over thither."* (Deuteronomy 34:4)

Why? Because Moses had become frustrated with the

people—always complaining, never content. They had already seen water flow from the rock once before, when God commanded Moses to strike it.

But this time, God gave a different command: not to strike the rock, but to speak to it (Numbers 20:7–12).

The Apostle Paul later wrote: *"…that Rock was Christ."* (1 Corinthians 10:4)

Christ was to be smitten once—at Calvary, not twice. Moses' disobedience, though it seemed small, carried a great cost.

He could see the land, but he could not enter. Moses died in the wilderness almost having made it but one thing stood in his way.

Almost obedience is disobedience. Almost persuaded is still lost. Almost reaching the finish line is not enough. Saul almost obeyed when he spared Agag. Israel almost entered when they turned back in unbelief. Agrippa was almost persuaded, but he remained unchanged. Moses almost crossed, but he fell short. The truth is simple and sobering: almost doesn't count with God.

The Ultimate Example

Jesus Christ carried obedience to its ultimate end. In Gethsemane He prayed: *"...nevertheless not as I will, but as thou wilt."* (Matthew 26:39) He humbled Himself and became *"obedient unto death, even the death of the cross."* (Philippians 2:8)

For the joy set before Him, He endured the cross, despising the shame, and is now set down at the right hand of God (Hebrews 12:2). His obedience brought salvation to all who believe: *"For as by one man's disobedience many were made sinners, so by the obedience of one shall many be made righteous."* (Romans 5:19)

Paul also lived faithfully to the end. Near his death he wrote: *"I have fought a good fight, I have finished my course, I have kept the faith: Henceforth there is laid up for me a crown of righteousness, which the Lord, the righteous judge, shall give me at that day: and not to me only, but unto all them also that love his appearing."* (2 Timothy 4:7–8)

The truth is clear. Starting is not enough. Almost is not enough. Obedience must be carried to the finish line.

The blessing, the provision, the miracle, and the eternal reward wait on the other side of full obedience.

- On that side,

  - Faith becomes sight,
  - promises become reality,
  - and the race of obedience ends with the crown of righteousness.

"For the wages of sin is death; but the gift of God is eternal life through Jesus Christ our Lord."

(Romans 6:23)

Chapter 3 – The Cost of Disobedience

Disobedience Has a Price

Disobedience always costs more than we expect. It promises pleasure but delivers pain; it offers freedom but ends in bondage.

The Lord's commandments are never meant to confine—they are meant to preserve. But when man rejects God's Word, he removes the very boundaries that keep him safe.

Paul wrote, *"For the wages of sin is death; but the gift of God is eternal life through Jesus Christ our Lord."* (Romans 6:23)

Sin always pays wages, and those wages are death—death to peace, death to purity, and, if unrepented of, death to the soul.

From Eden to Calvary, Scripture stands as a testimony that God means what He says. Every commandment ignored has a consequence attached to it. Every act of disobedience leaves a mark that cannot be erased except by repentance and blood.

Scripture gives us further warnings in other scenes as well.

Nadab and Abihu – Strange Fire in a Holy Place

In the book of Leviticus chapter 9, the glory of God had just descended. The tabernacle had been completed, and it gleamed in the wilderness.

Aaron and his sons had been consecrated, and fire had fallen from Heaven to consume the first sacrifice on the altar — proof that God Himself accepted their offering. The people shouted and fell on their faces as the presence of God filled the camp.

But moments later, fire became judgment.

Aaron's sons, Nadab and Abihu, took their censers and offered *"strange fire before the Lord, which He <u>commanded them not</u>."* (Leviticus 10:1)

Some think they took coals from the wrong source, entered at the wrong time, or acted under the influence of wine. However, the command concerning the Altar of Incense was clear: *"Ye shall offer no strange incense thereon."* (Exodus 30:9)

While the details may be uncertain, the fact is clear—they acted without command. And fire came out from before the Lord and consumed them.

They died where they were supposed to minister.

They were not pagans; they were priests—anointed, trained, and near to the presence of God. Yet disobedience in sacred duty brought sudden death.

It is a warning that the closer one stands to the altar, the more dangerous disobedience becomes.

In our day, "strange fire" burns in many churches—worship without holiness, ministry without submission, excitement without reverence.

It may glitter, but it does not glow with God's flame. True fire still falls only on true obedience.

The Lord still requires now what He required then: Do not offer what He has not commanded.

Israel's Rebellion in the Wilderness

The story of Israel in the wilderness is the story of a people who saw God's glory, yet still rebelled against His Word. They were not strangers to His presence—they walked under a cloud by day and fire by night. They ate manna that fell from Heaven and drank water that flowed from a rock. Yet despite daily miracles, they hardened their hearts against His command.

From the very beginning, obedience was the condition of blessing. God said, *"If ye will obey my voice indeed, and keep my covenant, then ye shall be a peculiar treasure unto me above all people."* (Exodus 19:5)

But when the test came, they murmured instead of trusting.

They cried out for deliverance, yet complained about the cost of freedom. They wanted the promise, but not the path that led there.

The same people who shouted when the Red Sea opened — doubted when the road grew long. The same lips that sang the song of Moses at the shore of deliverance murmured in the desert of discipline.

Disobedience doesn't always come with open rebellion—sometimes it starts with quiet complaint.

But every complaint questions the wisdom of God. Every murmur weakens faith. And soon, what began as grumbling becomes outright defiance.

The Test of Trust

At Kadesh-barnea, the people stood on the threshold of the Promised Land. Twelve spies went in to search the land. Ten returned with fear; two returned with faith. Yet Israel chose to believe the voice of fear.

"And all the congregation lifted up their voice, and cried; and the people wept that night... and said one to another, Let us make a captain, and let us return into Egypt." (Numbers 14:1–4)

They were one step away from the promise—yet they turned back. They saw the land. They heard the promise. But they would not obey.

What is wrong with us when we stand on the border of God's promise and still decide to turn back? After all the miracles He has performed in our lives—after every healing, every deliverance, every storm He has brought us through— how can we walk away? Yet we do it every day. It seems that at times we are more comfortable in bondage than in blessing, more at ease in misery than in deliverance.

Faith requires obedience even when the giants look bigger than the promise. Israel had witnessed the power of God in Egypt, but they could not trust the same God to give them Canaan.

The result was forty years of wandering. What could have been a short journey became a lifetime of delay.

Disobedience and unbelief in the Word of God and the promise of God will cost us a lifetime of delay.

One day we wake up and realize we have wasted so much time when it would have been easier, better, faster to just believe and obey.

We obey God in moments and see the joyful results of that obedience, yet afraid to fully commit.

Obeying God halfway is the same as not obeying at all. The history of Israel shows us that when faith falters, disobedience inevitably follows.

The Cost of Rebellion

In Numbers 16, Korah, Dathan, and Abiram rose up against Moses and Aaron, saying, *"Ye take too much upon you, seeing all the congregation are holy."* (v. 3)

They questioned divine authority, mistaking equality for anointing.

But the ground itself bore witness to God's displeasure. The earth opened, and the rebels were swallowed alive. Fire came out from the Lord and consumed two-hundred-fifty men who offered incense without command.

Though they were Levites, they were not priests.
All priests came from the tribe of Levi, but not all Levites were priests.
Only the sons of Aaron were authorized to burn incense before the Lord. Korah and his followers crossed a sacred line—they took holy fire into unholy hands. They tried to perform a priest's duty without a priest's calling. It was worship without obedience, service without submission, and it cost them their lives.

It is a fearful thing when man challenges the order of God. The same God who gave them freedom from Egypt demanded obedience.

Liberty without submission is rebellion.

"Now all these things happened unto them for ensamples: and they are written for our admonition, upon whom the ends of the world are come." (1 Corinthians 10:11)

Their story is not written to condemn, but to warn.

Israel's rebellion teaches us that spiritual privilege does not exempt us from obedience. You can walk under the cloud and still fall in the wilderness. You can eat heavenly manna and still miss the Promised Land. You can hear the voice of God and still die outside the promise—if you refuse to obey.

The Fire and the Glory

At Sinai, the people had seen fire descend upon the mountain. But the same fire that sanctified also consumed. When they made the golden calf, that same fire became judgment. God's presence is not only blessing—it is also boundary.

When Moses cried out for mercy, God answered, but not without consequence. *"As truly as I live, saith the Lord, all the earth shall be filled with the glory of the Lord."* (Numbers 14:21)

The glory of the Lord will fill the earth—with or without the obedience of men. Israel's disobedience did not cancel God's plan, but it cost them their place in it.

They stood at the border of promise, yet never crossed over. They came so close—but almost doesn't count. The generation that murmured died in the desert, and their children rose to take their place. Because they refused to believe in the promises of God and obey, an entire generation died in the wilderness.

The Lesson for Us

Israel's story is not ancient history—it is a mirror for today's church. God has not changed. His commands are still clear. His holiness is still holy. His altar is still sacred.

The closer we walk with God, the more exact our obedience must be. It is not that God accepts disobedience when you are far from Him; rather, the closer you draw, the more in tune with Him you must become.

The call to holiness, submission, and faith is not optional—it is the only path to the promise.

Disobedience will always delay destiny, but obedience will always open the door.

When we obey, we walk under the same cloud of glory that led Israel through the wilderness—the presence of God Himself. And when obedience is complete, the promise is sure.

Obedience is life. Disobedience is death. The choice remains.

"Create in me a clean heart, O God; and renew a right

spirit within me."

(Psalm 51:10)

Chapter 4 – The Spirit of Obedience

The Heart Behind the Command

The greatest test of obedience is not found in what we do, but in the spirit with which we do it.

True obedience flows out of faith and love, but false obedience springs from pride, fear, or self-interest. God not only measures the act, but also the attitude that produces it.

From the very beginning, the difference between those who pleased God and those who grieved Him was not only what they offered, but how and why they offered it.

Nowhere is this seen more clearly than in the story of Cain and Abel.

The Offering of Cain and Abel

The first recorded act of worship after Eden was not a song or a prayer—it was an offering.

"And in process of time it came to pass, that Cain brought of the fruit of the ground an offering unto the Lord. And Abel, he also brought of the firstlings of his flock and of the fat thereof. And the Lord had respect unto Abel and to his offering: But unto Cain and to his offering he had not respect." (Genesis 4:3–5)

At first glance, both men appear devoted. Both built an altar. Both brought a sacrifice. Both desired acceptance from God. Yet one found favor, and the other found rejection.

The reason? **Obedience.**

Abel offered according to divine revelation; Cain offered according to human reasoning. Abel's altar held blood; Cain's held produce. One came by faith; the other by flesh. Abel's worship was founded upon what God had shown;

59

Cain's worship was founded upon what he thought was
good enough.

The writer of Hebrews explains: *"By faith Abel offered unto God a more excellent sacrifice than Cain."* (Hebrews 11:4) Faith comes by hearing, and hearing by the Word of God (Romans 10:17). Somewhere between the garden and this altar, God had made His will known—that sin demanded a blood covering. Abel heard and obeyed. Cain heard and resisted.

Abel's lamb was more than a mere offering; it was a prophecy. It looked forward to Calvary, where the Lamb of God would be slain for the sins of the world.

Cain's fruits, though beautiful, lacked blood.
His altar was fragrant with labor, but it was void of life. He offered worship without repentance, effort without atonement, religion without relationship.

Obedience requires revelation, and revelation requires

humility. The carnal mind always prefers the work of its own hands, while faith always prefers the work of God's grace.

The Pattern in the Garden

To understand Cain's failure, we must look backward—to the garden where the pattern of obedience was first revealed.

When Adam and Eve sinned, they tried to cover themselves with fig leaves. But their handmade coverings could not erase their guilt. So the Lord, in mercy, did something profound: *"Unto Adam also and to his wife did the Lord God make coats of skins, and clothed them."* (Genesis 3:21)

To make those coats, blood had to be shed. The innocent died to cover the guilty. It was the first death in creation's history—a type and shadow of the Cross.

Revelation pulls back the curtain and declares that Jesus Christ is *"the Lamb slain from the foundation of the world."* (Revelation 13:8) The plan of redemption was not an afterthought; it was established before Adam ever drew his first breath.

God Himself set the precedent: acceptable worship would always require the shedding of innocent blood.

When Cain offered the fruit of the ground, he offered what God had already cursed. The ground had been cursed for Adam's sake (Genesis 3:17). The soil represented human labor under the weight of sin.

Abel, however, brought what God had sanctified—an offering that pointed to the coming Redeemer.

The difference between the two men was not simply their vocation, but their revelation.

Every altar since has been divided along the same line:

• Those who worship by revelation, and those who worship by reason.

• Those who seek to please God by faith, and those who seek to please Him by works.

• Those who obey what God has said, and those who offer what God never asked for.

The Spirit That Resists Correction

We live in a world that *resists* any form of correction — and I think we can all agree with that.

The flesh of humanity has grown out of control, completely given over to sin.

The spirit of the Antichrist is at work like never before—the spirit of lawlessness.

Homes without discipline.

Society without restraint.

Pulpits without rebuke.

It is a spirit that directly attacks the heart of God-a spirit of *resistance*. Yet it is no different now than it was then; all we must do is *submit to God*. Even after Cain's offering was rejected, God did not cast him away. The Lord reasoned with him tenderly, saying:

"If thou doest well, shalt thou not be accepted? and if thou doest not well, sin lieth at the door. And unto thee shall be his desire, and thou shalt rule over him." (Genesis 4:7)

Here we see divine mercy in action. God offered Cain a second chance. But instead of repentance, Cain chose resentment. Instead of humbling himself, he hardened himself. Instead of returning to the altar, he turned on his brother.

Pride silenced the call of grace.

The tragedy of Cain is that he wanted the reward of obedience without the surrender it required. He wanted divine favor without divine order. This is the danger of modern religion—man wants to come to God on his own terms. **But obedience does not negotiate. It submits.**

Disobedience is not born in the hands; it is conceived in the heart. The man who resists correction today will reject covenant tomorrow. The woman who stiffens at preaching will soon resist truth itself.

What starts as pride ends as separation.

Cain's rejection of correction birthed a curse that marked not only his body but his bloodline. When he walked away from the altar, he walked away from the presence of the Lord. And no man can worship God at a distance.

The Spirit of True Obedience

Abel's obedience, on the other hand, still speaks. Hebrews 11:4 says, *"By it he being dead yet speaketh."* His voice still echoes through Scripture, calling every generation back to the simplicity of pure obedience.

The spirit of obedience is not stubborn or self-serving—it is surrendered. It is not the performance of religion, but the posture of relationship. True obedience flows from faith, and faith flows from revelation.

The Apostle Paul captured it when he wrote, *"Let this mind be in you, which was also in Christ Jesus… who humbled himself, and became obedient unto death, even the death of the cross."* (Philippians 2:5–8)

Jesus did not obey out of compulsion; He obeyed because while living, He had already crucified the will of the flesh and submitted it to the will of God. His obedience was not reluctant but joyful: *"Lo, I come to do thy will, O God."*

(Hebrews 10:9)

That is the essence of holiness—obedience that springs from love, not fear. Holiness is not bondage; it is belonging. It is not restriction; it is relationship. It is the soul saying, *"Lord, not my will, but Thine be done."*

The spirit of true obedience does not count the cost—it sees the cross and follows anyway.

The Purity of Obedience

Two altars still stand before every believer:
- One built by Cain—of self-will and self-righteousness.
- One built by Abel—of surrender and sacrifice.
- One is beautiful but lifeless.
- The other is bloody but accepted.

The difference between the two is not the materials, but the motive.

We must be careful that our worship does not become Cain's altar—busy, impressive, and fruitless.

We can build programs, sing songs, and even preach sermons that God never asked for. We can give offerings that cost us time but not tears, money but not repentance, effort but not obedience.

But the fire of God still only falls on what He commands.

Abel's altar still burns. His obedience still speaks. And his faith still testifies that the only worship God receives is the kind that He Himself has prescribed.

When we come to God in true obedience, heaven always responds. When we lay down our will, His fire falls upon our sacrifice.

And though the world may not understand our altar, it is on that altar that we find peace, presence, and power.

But what happens when obedience is demanded not of the strong, but of the trembling? When God calls the weakest man in Israel and names him mighty? That is where the spirit of obedience becomes the strength of obedience.

"And he said unto me, My grace is sufficient for thee: for my strength is made perfect in weakness."

(2 Corinthians 12:9)

Chapter 5 – Obedience in Weakness

The Call in the Winepress

When the angel of the Lord found Gideon, he was not standing on a battlefield—he was hiding in a winepress. Israel had been overrun by Midian; their fields were stripped, their barns emptied, and their courage stolen. The people cried for deliverance, yet they cowered in fear.

"And there came an angel of the Lord, and sat under an oak which was in Ophrah… and his son Gideon threshed wheat by the winepress, to hide it from the Midianites." (Judges 6:11)

It was there, in the quiet of fear, that God called him.

The Lord looked upon Gideon—not the warrior he wished he was, but the man he was becoming—and said, *"The Lord is with thee, thou mighty man of valour."* (Judges 6:12)

At first, those words made no sense. Gideon was no warrior; he was a survivor. He was threshing wheat in secret so his family could eat. Yet Heaven called him mighty.

That is where obedience begins:

not in our strength, but in His word. God does not call the qualified; He qualifies the called. When the Lord calls something what it has not yet become, His word carries the power to make it so.

As it is written: *"(God) calleth those things which be not as though they were."* (Romans 4:17)

Gideon answered the call with hesitation. *"O my Lord, if the Lord be with us, why then is all this befallen us? and where be all his miracles which our fathers told us of… but now the Lord hath*

forsaken us, and delivered us into the hands of the Midianites."
(Judges 6:13)

Like so many of us, Gideon's problem was not doubt in God's ability—but doubt in God's attention. He could believe that God had worked miracles, but he struggled to believe that God would do it now.

Yet the Lord did not argue theology; He simply redirected Gideon's focus. *"Go in this thy might, and thou shalt save Israel from the hand of the Midianites: have not I sent thee?"* (Judges 6:14)

Notice, God called Gideon to go in his own might—not because Gideon was strong, but because God had placed something divine inside his weakness. That is the secret of obedience: the strength to act is often hidden in the very places we feel least capable.

Gideon replied, *"O my Lord, wherewith shall I save Israel? behold, my family is poor in Manasseh, and I am the least in my father's house."* (Judges 6:15)

To God, that was the point. He specializes in beginning His greatest works through the smallest vessels. He chose the weak to confound the mighty, the foolish to confound the wise, so that no flesh should glory in His presence.

When Gideon looked at his inadequacy, God looked at his availability. When Gideon saw a frightened man, God saw a willing one.

Obedience doesn't always look courageous—it often looks like a trembling "yes." It's not confidence in self; it's trust in the One who called.

"Surely I will be with thee, and thou shalt smite the Midianites as one man." (Judges 6:16)

That promise changed everything. When the Lord said, "Surely I will be with thee," He placed divine partnership behind Gideon's obedience. The presence of God would do what Gideon could never do.

From that moment, Gideon built an altar and named it Jehovah-shalom – The Lord is Peace (Judges 6:24). It was a declaration that even in fear, he had found calm through obedience.

He still had questions, still had doubts—but he now had peace enough to act. Obedience doesn't wait for every question to be answered; it moves when God speaks.

The Test of Obedience

Before Gideon ever faced Midian, he first had to face his own household. God's first command was not to fight the enemy in the field—but to tear down the idol in his father's backyard.

"And it came to pass the same night, that the Lord said unto him,

Take thy father's young bullock, even the second bullock of seven years old, and throw down the altar of Baal that thy father hath, and cut down the grove that is by it: and build an altar unto the Lord thy God upon the top of this rock." (Judges 6:25–26)

Before God could use Gideon to deliver a nation, He had to teach him that obedience begins at home. Public victories are built on private altars. The battle for a generation begins in secret places of surrender.

Gideon obeyed, but he did it by night. *"Then Gideon took ten men of his servants, and did as the Lord had said unto him: and so it was, because he feared his father's household, and the men of the city, that he could not do it by day, that he did it by night."* (Judges 6:27)

He was afraid—but he still obeyed. That's what God honors. Fear does not disqualify you from obedience; disobedience does. Gideon's nighttime obedience became the proof of his calling.

When morning came, the townsmen saw the altar of Baal torn down, the grove destroyed, and a new altar standing in its place. They were enraged and demanded Gideon's death.

But something remarkable happened—Gideon's father, Joash, who had once permitted idolatry, suddenly defended his son. *"Will ye plead for Baal? ... if he be a god, let him plead for himself."* (Judges 6:31)

When one man obeyed, courage awakened in another. That is the power of obedience—it is contagious.

God often tests us with small commands before He trusts us with great ones. Before the walls of Jericho fell, Israel had to march in silence. Before Elijah called down fire on Mount Carmel, he had to rebuild the altar. Before Gideon could face an army, he had to destroy an idol.

Obedience always begins with the unseen test—the quiet surrender that nobody applauds. It's not the size of the act, but the spirit behind it that God measures.

In this moment, Gideon learned something eternal: God cannot fight for you until you've surrendered what fights against Him. You cannot win a public war while protecting a private idol.

So the Lord tore down Gideon's fear one command at a time. Each act of obedience stripped away another layer of insecurity. Every altar he built replaced something that had once enslaved him.

The man who trembled in a winepress was becoming a man who could stand before armies.

The Reduction

Obedience will always lead to a moment when God starts taking things away. It's not punishment—it's preparation.

When Gideon gathered his army to face Midian, thirty-two thousand men answered the call. It must have felt like confirmation. For the first time, the numbers were on his side. But then God spoke words no general wants to hear:

"The people that are with thee are too many for me to give the Midianites into their hands, lest Israel vaunt themselves against me, saying, Mine own hand hath saved me." (Judges 7:2)

Too many. That's not what Gideon expected to hear. But God was never interested in victory by statistics. He was interested in glory by surrender.

The Lord told Gideon, *"Proclaim in the ears of the people, saying, Whosoever is fearful and afraid, let him return and depart early from mount Gilead."* (Judges 7:3)

And twenty-two thousand men went home. Only ten thousand remained.

The first reduction removed fear. God will always separate

the fearful before the faithful can advance. Faith and fear cannot march together—they will always pull in opposite directions. Yet even after this, God said again, *"The people are yet too many."*

Ten thousand seemed small, but Heaven said it was still too big.

So Gideon led them to the water. There the Lord performed a strange test: *"Every one that lappeth of the water with his tongue, as a dog lappeth, him shalt thou set by himself; likewise every one that boweth down upon his knees to drink."* (Judges 7:5)

Only three hundred men lifted the water to their mouths with their hands. They stayed alert while others bowed low. They were cautious in the simplest moment.

And God said, *"By the three hundred men that lapped will I save you."* (Judges 7:7)

When Gideon watched the multitudes walk away, something

inside him had to tremble. The odds went from four to one, to thirteen to one, to four hundred fifty to one. Every natural measure of success was gone—but that's when supernatural victory begins.

Obedience will always reduce what you depend on until all that's left is faith. God didn't want Gideon to win with strength; He wanted him to win with surrender.

We learn the same lesson every time God narrows our options, drains our resources, or takes away what made us feel secure. He is not forsaking us; He is focusing us. He is teaching us to depend on His word, not our weapons.

The Lord said to Paul centuries later, *"My strength is made perfect in weakness."* (2 Corinthians 12:9) The same truth lived in Gideon's story: God's power shines brightest when man's strength fades away.

The Victory of the Few

When Gideon stood overlooking the valley of Midian, it must have seemed impossible. The Midianite army filled the plain *"like grasshoppers for multitude,"* and their camels were *"without number"* (Judges 7:12). Below him stretched a sea of tents, torches, and weapons—men as far as the eye could see. Above him stood only three hundred.

But the Lord was still speaking. God had already done His separating. He had trimmed away the fearful and the faithless. What remained was pure obedience.

That night, the Lord gave Gideon a final word of assurance: *"Arise, get thee down unto the host; for I have delivered it into thine hand."* (Judges 7:9)
But knowing Gideon's heart, God added something gracious: *"But if thou fear to go down, go thou with Phurah thy servant down to the host: and thou shalt hear what they say; and afterward shall thine hands be strengthened."* (Judges 7:10–11)

When Gideon crept near the enemy camp, he overheard two men speaking: one told a dream of a barley cake tumbling into the host of Midian and overturning a tent. His companion interpreted it, saying, *"This is nothing else save the sword of Gideon the son of Joash, a man of Israel: for into his hand hath God delivered Midian."* (Judges 7:14)

The enemy had more confidence in Gideon's calling than Gideon did himself. When he heard it, Scripture says, *"he worshipped."* (Judges 7:15) That's the heart of obedience: before the battle ever begins, the worshiper bows in faith.

Gideon returned to his men and gave the strangest command an army has ever heard. No swords drawn. No spears lifted. Each man held a trumpet in one hand and a clay pitcher in the other. Inside the pitcher burned a hidden torch.

When the signal came, they broke the pitchers, lifted their lights, blew the trumpets, and cried, *"The sword of the Lord, and of Gideon!"* (Judges 7:20)

The valley erupted in confusion. The Midianites turned their swords against each other and fled in panic. Without ever swinging a weapon, Israel won the battle.

It was obedience—not manpower—that brought the victory. When the pitchers broke, the light shone forth; when obedience broke the vessel, the glory was revealed.

That is still how God works today. Our weakness becomes His weapon. Our surrender becomes His strategy. When the flesh is broken, the light of the Holy Ghost shines through.

This was not just Gideon's story—it is the pattern of every believer. We may not face Midianite armies, but we face doubt, fear, and the limits of our own ability. And God still calls us to obedience when the odds are against us. He still says, *"Go in this thy might."*

Every great revival, every miracle, every deliverance begins with someone willing to obey against the odds.

The weapons of Gideon's 300 were not their strength, but their submission. They followed divine strategy even when it defied logic. They obeyed a command that made no sense — and it unleashed Heaven's power.

Today, God still reduces armies to reveal His glory. He still breaks vessels to let His light shine. He still honors obedience above ability.

The same God who spoke to Gideon speaks to the church:

"Not by might, nor by power, but by my spirit, saith the Lord of hosts." (Zechariah 4:6)

When the church obeys in weakness, it moves in power. When the people of God lay down their own plans, the fire of Heaven falls again.

Gideon began in fear but ended in faith. He started in hiding but finished in victory. Every step of obedience transformed his weakness into strength.

The story of Gideon proves that obedience is not about power—it is about partnership. God does not need our perfection; He needs our participation. When we obey, He does the rest.

"Be thou faithful unto death, and I will give thee a crown of life."

(Revelation 2:10)

Chapter 6 – Obedience and Eternal Reward

The Promise of Reward

Every act of obedience carries a promise beyond what eyes can see. God never calls a man or woman to obey without attaching a divine outcome. His commands are not to rob us of joy, but to lead us into glory.

Jesus said plainly, *"If ye love me, keep my commandments."* (John 14:15) And then He added the reward: *"I will not leave you comfortless: I will come to you."* (John 14:18)

Obedience opens the door to divine presence. The world sees commandments as burdens, but the child of God sees them as invitations. Each commandment is an open door into deeper fellowship with the Lord.

From the beginning, God has tied obedience to reward:

- Adam's obedience would have preserved Eden forever.
- Abraham's obedience brought a covenant that still blesses generations.
- Moses' obedience brought a nation out of bondage.
- The Apostles' obedience birthed the Church through the power of the Holy Ghost.

Every promise in Scripture rests on the foundation of obedience. And every disobedience forfeits what obedience would have gained.

"If ye be willing and obedient, ye shall eat the good of the land." (Isaiah 1:19)

The will of God is always followed by the reward of God, though the timing belongs to Him alone. Obedience may not pay immediately, but it always pays eventually.

When Peter asked what reward would come to those who had left all to follow Christ, Jesus answered: *"Verily I say unto you, There is no man that hath left house, or parents, or brethren, or wife, or children, for the kingdom of God's sake, who shall not*

receive manifold more in this present time, and in the world to come

life everlasting." (Luke 18:29–30)

In other words, no obedient act is ever wasted. Heaven keeps perfect records. Every sacrifice, every prayer, every act of surrender will find its reward either here or in eternity.

The Book of Hebrews echoes this truth: *"For God is not unrighteous to forget your work and labour of love, which ye have shewed toward his name."* (Hebrews 6:10)

God cannot forget obedience. He does not ignore faithfulness. Even when man overlooks it, Heaven remembers.

The reward of obedience is not always material—it is often spiritual:
• The peace that follows surrender.
• The anointing that rests on holiness.
• The presence that fills a life yielded to God.

• The joy that overflows from knowing you have pleased the Lord.

Earthly treasures fade, but spiritual rewards endure. The obedient man may not always be rich, but he will never be empty. He carries a peace the world cannot take away and a hope the world cannot understand.

The Faithful Endure

Obedience is not proven in a single act—it is measured across a lifetime. Faith that obeys for a season will fail in the storm, but faith that endures to the end secures the crown.

Jesus said, *"He that shall endure unto the end, the same shall be saved."* (Matthew 24:13) Endurance is the test of genuine obedience. It is easy to obey when the voice of God is fresh and the promise feels near; it is harder when Heaven is silent and the path grows dark.

The Bible is filled with those who began well but refused to finish. King Saul obeyed partially and was rejected. Demas followed Paul for a season, but love for this present world drew him away. Even Israel, after walking under the cloud and passing through the sea, died in the wilderness because their obedience was short-lived.

It is not how we start that Heaven measures—it is how we finish.

The Apostle Paul, nearing the end of his journey, looked back and said, *"I have fought a good fight, I have finished my course, I have kept the faith."* (2 Timothy 4:7) He had faced prison, persecution, hunger, shipwreck, betrayal, and pain, but none of it could turn him aside. Obedience anchored him when nothing else could.

Paul's life teaches us that obedience must be stronger than emotion. There were days when faith had no feeling, when prayers brought no answer, and when the cost of following Christ seemed unbearable. Yet he pressed on, not because it was easy, but because obedience had become his nature.

That is what the Holy Ghost produces in the yielded soul—a steadfastness that refuses to quit, a determination that endures even when weary, and a love for God that is stronger than the pull of the world.

The faithful endure not because they are flawless, but because they are surrendered. They have learned that failure is not final when repentance is real. They rise again, dust themselves off, and keep walking in the path of obedience.

Proverbs declares, *"A just man falleth seven times, and riseth up again."* (Proverbs 24:16)

Enduring obedience is not perfection—it is persistence. It is the heart that says, *"Though He slay me, yet will I trust in Him."* (Job 13:15)

Hebrews 10:36 reminds us, *"For ye have need of patience, that, after ye have done the will of God, ye might receive the promise."*

Patience is obedience that waits. It is faith stretched over time. It does not demand instant reward—it trusts God's timing.

The faithful endure because they see something others cannot see. They look beyond the weariness of today to the joy that is set before them. They run with patience, knowing that every mile of obedience brings them closer to eternal reward.

The Crown of Obedience

The finish line of faith is not the grave—it is glory. Obedience does not end when life does; it continues into eternity as reward. Every act of faithfulness on earth becomes treasure in Heaven.

The Apostle Paul declared, *"Henceforth there is laid up for me a crown of righteousness, which the Lord, the righteous judge, shall give me at that day: and not to me only, but unto all them also that love his appearing."* (2 Timothy 4:8)

That verse does not speak of achievement—it speaks of endurance. Paul's reward was not for preaching alone, but for finishing. He endured until obedience became victory, and that victory became his crown.

Scripture speaks of several crowns:

• The crown of righteousness for those who finish in faith (2 Timothy 4:8).

• The crown of life for those who endure temptation (James 1:12; Revelation 2:10).

• The incorruptible crown for those who discipline their walk (1 Corinthians 9:25).

• The crown of glory for those who shepherd faithfully (1 Peter 5:4).

• The crown of rejoicing for those who win souls (1 Thessalonians 2:19).

Though their names differ, every crown is rooted in the same soil—obedience. It is not talent that earns them, nor title, nor position. It is faithfulness to God's Word until the end.

Heaven's reward system is not based on visible success. Some of the greatest crowns will belong to people whose names were never known on earth—the praying mother, the faithful elder, the intercessor who labored unseen, the saint who quietly carried the burdens of others.

God measures greatness not by applause but by obedience. He sees the hidden sacrifices, the midnight prayers, the silent battles, and every unseen "yes" spoken in the shadow of His will.

When Jesus returns, the Bible says, *"Behold, I come quickly; and my reward is with me, to give every man according as his work shall be."* (Revelation 22:12)

That word *reward* literally means wage—but in Heaven's economy it isn't payment for merit, it is proof of remembrance. It is a witness that God never forgets obedience.

Every crown will testify to a story of surrender. Each jewel will represent a moment of obedience when quitting would have been easier. And when those crowns are placed in the hands of the Redeemed, the redeemed will not wear them in pride—they will cast them before the throne, saying, *"Thou art worthy, O Lord, to receive glory and honour and power."* (Revelation 4:11)

The crown of obedience is not for our exaltation but for His. Our reward is not in recognition—it is in revelation. We will see Him as He is, and every sacrifice will seem small in the light of His glory.

The Eternal Perspective

Obedience has never been about the moment—it has always been about eternity. Every act of surrender is an investment beyond this life. When we obey, we trade what is temporary for what is eternal.

The saints of old understood this. They lived as strangers and pilgrims in the earth, seeking *"a city which hath foundations, whose builder and maker is God."* (Hebrews 11:10) They obeyed not because it was convenient, but because they saw something invisible—something greater than comfort, greater than gain.

Moses *"refused to be called the son of Pharaoh's daughter; choosing rather to suffer affliction with the people of God, than to enjoy the pleasures of sin for a season."* (Hebrews 11:24–25) Why? Because *"he had respect unto the recompence of the reward."* (v. 26)

He looked ahead. He saw beyond the palace, beyond the gold, beyond the moment. His obedience was driven by an eternal vision.

The carnal mind obeys for what it can gain; the spiritual mind obeys for who it will see. The reward of obedience is not merely a crown—it is communion. To see Jesus, the One who was obedient unto death, to walk in the light of His glory forever—that is the highest reward of all.

When faith has run its course and obedience has finished its race, the faithful will hear those long-awaited words: *"Well done, thou good and faithful servant: thou hast been faithful over a few things, I will make thee ruler over many things: enter thou into the joy of thy lord."* (Matthew 25:21)

That single sentence will outweigh every sacrifice, every tear, every trial. To hear *"Well done"* from the mouth of the Master is worth a lifetime of obedience.

The eternal perspective changes everything. It reminds us that:

- Obedience is not wasted—it is stored.
- Sacrifice is not loss—it is investment.
- Delay is not denial—it is preparation.
- Suffering is not the end—it is the pathway to glory.

Paul wrote, *"For our light affliction, which is but for a moment, worketh for us a far more exceeding and eternal weight of glory."* (2

Corinthians 4:17)

Every act of obedience here builds weight there—glory accumulating beyond what time can measure. The life of the obedient is never lost in obscurity; it is hidden in eternity.

When the last trumpet sounds, when the graves give up their dead and the faithful rise incorruptible, obedience will stand as Heaven's testimony.

Every step, every yes, every tear will become part of a story that ends in triumph. The obedient will walk streets of gold not because they were perfect, but because they submitted to the perfect will of God.

The reward of obedience is not just Heaven—it is Him. To see Jesus face to face, to behold the Lamb who was slain, to stand complete in His presence, washed, redeemed, and victorious—that is the other side of obedience.

"Let us hear the conclusion of the whole matter: Fear God, and keep his commandments: for this is the whole duty of man."

(Ecclesiastes 12:13)

Final Benediction:

Let this truth rest deep within your spirit:

Obedience is not the loss of your will—it is the discovery of His.

It is the place where your "yes" meets His purpose, where surrender becomes strength, and where submission unlocks communion with the Almighty.

Every command is an invitation into His presence.
Every act of obedience is a step closer to His heart.
When you say "yes" in weakness, Heaven leans near in power.
When you yield in silence, the voice of God begins to speak again.

Maybe as you've read these pages, the Holy Ghost has whispered something to you—some unfinished call, some delayed surrender, some quiet nudge of conviction.
Do not turn it away. Do not reason it out.
Obey it. Even if it costs you comfort, even if it costs you pride, obey.

For on the other side of obedience is the life you've been praying for.

There will come a day when every struggle will end—when faith becomes sight, and obedience becomes worship. In that moment, as you stand before the throne and behold the face of the One who called you, you will finally understand: every sacrifice was small compared to His glory; every "yes" was worth it all.

So walk humbly. Obey quickly. Love deeply.
Let nothing steal the joy of pleasing the One who purchased you with His own blood.
And when the road feels long, remember—He is still guiding every step, waiting on the other side of your obedience with arms open wide.

For in the end, the reward at the finish line of obedience is not a crown, but Jesus Christ Himself.

Acknowledgments

First and foremost, I give glory to the Lord Jesus Christ, whose mercy called me, whose grace kept me, and whose voice still speaks through obedience. Every page in this book exists because of His patience and presence. Without Him, there would be no message to write and no strength to finish it.

To my wife, **Heather**, whose unwavering love and prayerful support carried me through this journey — you are the quiet strength behind every word. Your faith has been both anchor and inspiration, and I thank God every day for your partnership in life and ministry.

To my **Pastor, Kenneth Harman**, thank you for your guidance, example, and steadfast leadership. Your love for truth, your faithfulness to God's Word, and your investment in my life have helped shape the message within these pages. I am grateful for your covering, your counsel, and your constant encouragement to walk in obedience to the call of God.

To my family, friends, and church family who have believed in me, encouraged me, and prayed for me — your faithfulness has reminded me that obedience is never walked alone.

To every saint, minister, and mentor who has poured into my life over the years — your example has shown me what it means to serve with humility, holiness, and conviction.

Finally, to the readers who open these pages with hungry hearts — may the words within draw you closer to the One who still rewards obedience. Every prayer whispered while writing was for you.

All glory to the One who is worthy of it all.

— **Larry M. Treat**